SUPER SCIENCE LAB

BRIGHT IDEAS

Contents

Read all about **rainbows** on page 32.

You'll need a **3V battery** for most of the experiments in this book.

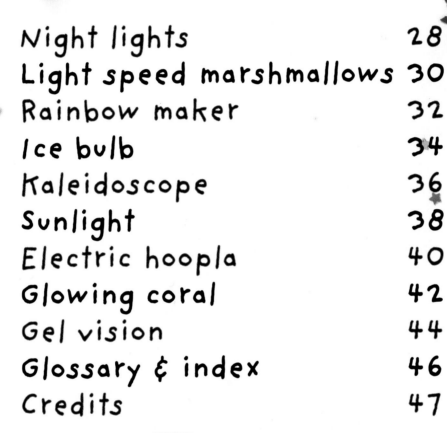

How fast does light travel from the **Sun**? Check out pages 38-39.

What's inside your **eyes**? The answer's on pages 22-23!

What's going on inside an **LED**? Turn the page to find out.

Shine on!

In the pack on the front of this book you'll find some **LEDs**, which you can use in all kinds of experiments. Here's the lowdown on how these **SMALL** but **MIGHTY** lights work and what they're used for.

These pins carry electricity from a power source to the LED.

LED STANDS FOR light-emitting diode. These tiny bulbs come in a wide range of colors and shapes. They're tougher and brighter than ordinary light bulbs, and very energy efficient.

IN AN LED, electricity releases light as it passes through a semiconductor made of silicon. Silicon conducts electricity rather poorly, but if certain other chemicals are added, electricity can flow in one direction (this is called semi-conduction). Depending on the chemicals chosen, the electrons traveling across the semiconductor give off different colored light.

THE FIRST LED was created in the 1920s by unsung Russian genius Oleg Vladimirovich Losev.

INFRARED EXPERIMENT
Your TV remote control uses an infrared LED to send signals to your TV or VCR. Infrared is normally invisible to human eyes. But here's how you can see the LED light up: look at it through the viewfinder of the camera on a cell phone, which is sensitive to infrared.

6

MULTICOLORED LEDS can be made into beautiful, vibrant displays. The screens of giant outdoor televisions are made up of millions of LEDs.

LED SPOTTING There are probably dozens of LEDs in your home—if you know where to find them. The on/off light on electronic equipment is usually an LED. Modern computer mice use LEDs on their bottoms to sense movement. Remote controls use LEDs, too. See how many LEDs you can find around the house.

The light from an LED is concentrated in a single direction by reflective internal walls.

SPECIALLY ARRANGED LEDS can spell out words and numbers or light up simple pictures. If you look closely, you can see the individual LEDs on modern crosswalk lights.

Glowy throwies

These little decorations are a fun way to **BRIGHTEN UP** metal surfaces. And they're **SUPER EASY** to make. Just follow these instructions, then toss your throwies onto your fridge door and watch them glow!

WARNING
Never use a battery with the wrong voltage! All the experiments in this book use three-volt batteries.

HOW TO MAKE A THROWY

These are called pins.

1. Slide the battery between the pins of an LED, so that the longer pin touches the positive terminal, which is usually marked with a +.

2. Wrap some adhesive tape tightly around the pins of the LED.

3. Tape a small magnet over the positive terminal of the battery.

4. Gently toss your glowy throwy a short distance onto a metallic surface.

Grab these:

An LED

A small magnet

3V battery

Colorful adhesive tape

How does it work?

A glowy throwy is a very simple **electrical circuit**. In a circuit, an energy source like a battery **pushes** electrons around in a loop.

The electrons travel from one part of the battery, called the **negative terminal**, to another part, called the **positive terminal**.

As the electrons pass through the LED, they release **light**.

Throwies were invented by a group of New York-based artists as a friendly, fun alternative to spray-paint graffiti.

They look awesome outside in the dark— but remember that you'll need to take them home to dispose of the batteries correctly.

Light lines

These sparkling optical fibers may look **PRETTY**, but they're also **POWERFUL** technology. Information in the form of flashing light can be sent racing through them, like super fast **MORSE CODE**. A single fiber, the width of a human hair, can carry 300 million phone calls at once!

Flashy light

LIGHT UP YOUR NIGHT with this flashlight. It's great for reading comic books under the covers. And you can switch it off fast when Mom comes in to see if you're asleep...

Grab these:

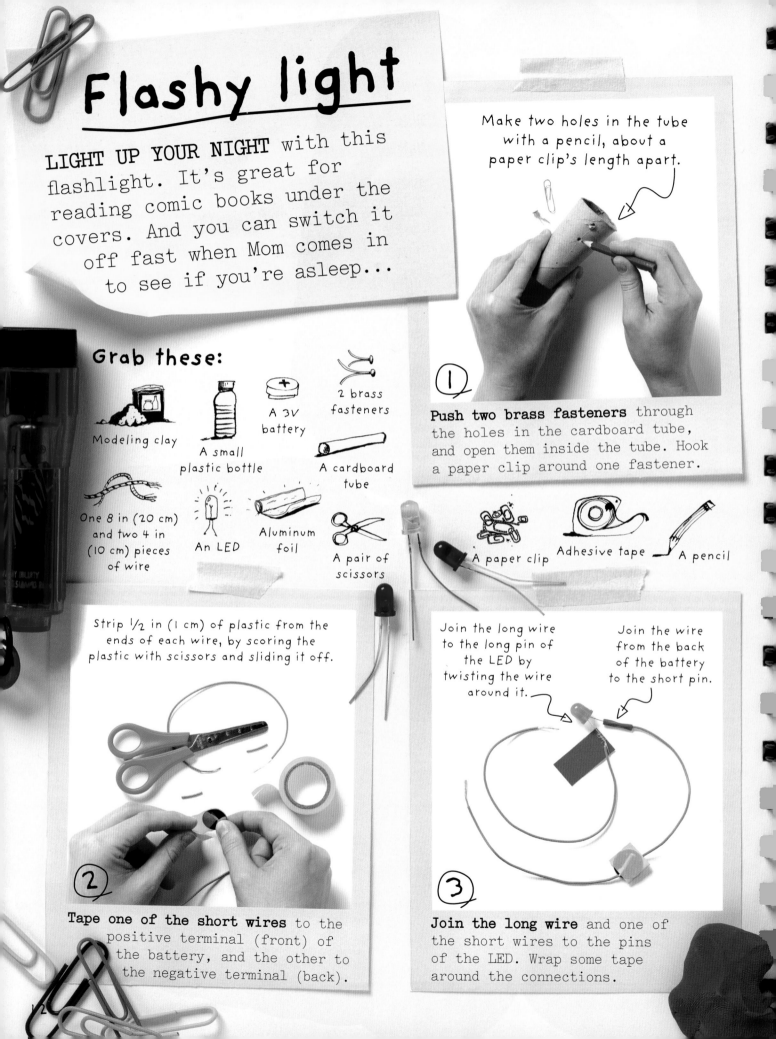

Modeling clay

A small plastic bottle

A 3V battery

2 brass fasteners

A cardboard tube

One 8 in (20 cm) and two 4 in (10 cm) pieces of wire

An LED

Aluminum foil

A pair of scissors

A paper clip

Adhesive tape

A pencil

Make two holes in the tube with a pencil, about a paper clip's length apart.

① **Push two brass fasteners** through the holes in the cardboard tube, and open them inside the tube. Hook a paper clip around one fastener.

Strip ½ in (1 cm) of plastic from the ends of each wire, by scoring the plastic with scissors and sliding it off.

② **Tape one of the short wires** to the positive terminal (front) of the battery, and the other to the negative terminal (back).

Join the long wire to the long pin of the LED by twisting the wire around it.

Join the wire from the back of the battery to the short pin.

③ **Join the long wire** and one of the short wires to the pins of the LED. Wrap some tape around the connections.

Tape over the wires and fasteners to make them secure.

④ **Connect one of the wires** to a brass fastener inside the tube. Connect the other wire to the other fastener.

The LED should sit at the base of the cone.

⑤ Push the bottle top into the tube; secure with tape.

Cut the top off of the bottle and cover it with foil. Pull the LED through the neck of the bottle and fix it in place with modeling clay.

The reflective foil directs light outward.

Make sure the battery doesn't touch the foil inside the flashlight.

How does it work?

Electricity is the flow of tiny charged specks of matter called electrons. When the two terminals of a battery are joined together by a loop of wire, electrons are **pushed** into the wire at the negative terminal and **drawn back** out at the positive terminal.

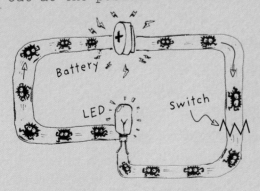

Battery

LED

Switch

A switch is just a break in the circuit. The electrons can't jump the gap if the switch is open, so the LED won't light up.

You can decorate your flashlight with colored paper, markers, or stickers.

SWITCH ON the flashlight by moving the paper clip so it makes contact with the other fastener.

13

Flying colors

Wouldn't the world look dull in black and white? Happily, most of us can see a wide range of colors, from radiant **REDS** to vibrant **VIOLETS**. But here's a question: what exactly **IS** color?

LIGHT TRAVELS in waves, like ripples on the surface of a lake. Light waves can be closely packed together or widely spaced out. We see different lengths of light waves as different colors. All of these colors together are called the *VISIBLE SPECTRUM*.

RED LIGHT has the longest wavelength of the visible spectrum, and violet light has the **shortest**. The other colors—orange, yellow, green, blue, and indigo—come somewhere in between.

THE VISIBLE SPECTRUM

A **WAVELENGTH** is the distance between the peaks of two waves.

14

If an object reflects red light, but absorbs all the other colors, then only red light will reach our eyes, so we see (you guessed it!) red.

Now I'm seeing red!

Light

THIS WRITING absorbs all colors of light, which is why it looks black. If something REFLECTS all colors of light, it looks white—like the paper this is written on.

When light waves hit an object, they either bounce off it or are absorbed. When we look at an object, we see the light that reflects from that object into our eyes.

SOME ANIMALS CAN SEE COLORS that are invisible to us humans. Bees can see ultraviolet. The centers of these flowers look dark—but only if you can see UV.

NOT EVERYONE CAN SEE THE EYE IN THIS CIRCLE. That's because **color-blind** people can't tell the difference between colors like red and green, or blue and yellow.

15

Crystal creations

You don't need a green thumb to grow your own **CRYSTAL GARDEN**. In fact, you don't need much time either, since this garden grows overnight! Simply hang your crystal creations in a window, and they'll sparkle in the sunlight.

Grab these:

Pipe cleaners

Alum*

Glass jar

Tea kettle

Teaspoon

Paper clips

Pencil

HOW TO MAKE CRYSTALS

1. Make a shape out of pipe cleaners. It needs to be smaller than the opening of your jar. Twist a paper clip into an S-shape. Hook it onto your pipe-cleaner shape.

2. Boil water in a tea kettle. Pour it into the jar.

3. Add alum, a teaspoon at a time, until no more will dissolve. Stir after each spoonful.

4. Balance the pencil across the top of the jar. Hang your shape from the pencil into the solution.

5. Leave the jar overnight. The next morning, crystals will have appeared!

*You'll find alum with the spices in grocery stores.

How does it work?

When you stir alum into hot water, you're making a solution. But hot water can hold more alum as a solution than cold water. So when the water begins to cool, there's less space for the alum that's dissolved in it. Some of the alum is forced out of the solution, and it gradually joins together in solid crystals.

Make sure you pour the extra crystal growing solution down the sink, so that nobody accidentally drinks it!

GLOWING CRYSTALS
To make glowing crystals, paint the pipe cleaners with glow-in-the-dark paint. Let the paint dry before putting the pipe cleaners in the alum solution.

EVEN MORE CRYSTAL EXPERIMENTS
You can also make crystals by dissolving SUGAR, SALT, or EPSOM SALTS in hot water. Follow the method on page 16, but swap the alum for one of these other ingredients. And be patient—these alternative crystals take several days to grow.

YOU COULD MAKE A CRYSTAL MOBILE!

17

All that glitters

The secret of a crystal's sparkle is in its **SHAPE**. These **QUARTZ CRYSTALS** grow in regular patterns with flat faces. If light hits a face at a shallow angle, it **BOUNCES OFF**, like a stone skipping across water. But if it enters a crystal, it reflects off the structure inside, making the crystal sparkle.

Alien metal detectors

These cute little creatures are on a **METAL FINDING MISSION**. If you touch their hands or antennae to a metal object, their **LED NOSES** light up with excitement!

Grab these:

Some aluminum foil

A 3V battery

Some modeling clay

Three pieces of wire 6 in (15 cm), 8 in (20 cm), and 2 in (5 cm) long

An LED

Scissors

Adhesive tape

Connect the medium wire to the positive terminal.

Connect the shortest wire to the negative terminal.

① **Strip ½ in (1 cm) of plastic** from each end of the three wires with some scissors. Then tape the two shorter wires to the battery.

Wrap the end of the SHORT wire around the SHORT pin of the LED.

Battery

② Wrap the end of the LONG wire around the LONG pin.

Wrap the ends of the short and long wires around the short and long pins of the LED, and tape them in place.

If you touch these wires together the LED should light up.

③ **Wrap some modeling clay** around the wires connected to the LED, leaving the LED itself sticking out.

Touch an object with these "SENSOR HANDS" to test it.

We're hunting for metal!

NOW you can decorate your creature with eyes, feet, and other features.

(4)

Wrap some more modeling clay around the battery. Then squash some aluminum foil into balls around the ends of each wire.

(5)

Try touching your creature's hands to various different objects, like keys, coins, and spoons. Does his nose light up?

How does it work?

It's easy for electricity to flow through some materials—those substances are called **conductors**. Metals are very good conductors, which is why the insides of wires are made of metal. Other materials, like plastics, barely let electricity through them at all. Those are called **insulators**.

When you touch both of the arms or antennae of your metal detector creature to a conductor, you're completing an electrical circuit between the two terminals of the battery. Electricity flows around the circuit, through the wires and the conductor. As it passes through the **LED**, it makes the LED light up.

21

Look out!

CAN YOU BELIEVE YOUR EYES? This astonishing image shows the surface of a retina—the layer at the back of an eyeball—under a powerful microscope. The wiggly gray and purple shapes are the light-sensing cells that you use to see the world around you.

This is a cone cell.

You have three different types of cone cell in your eyes.

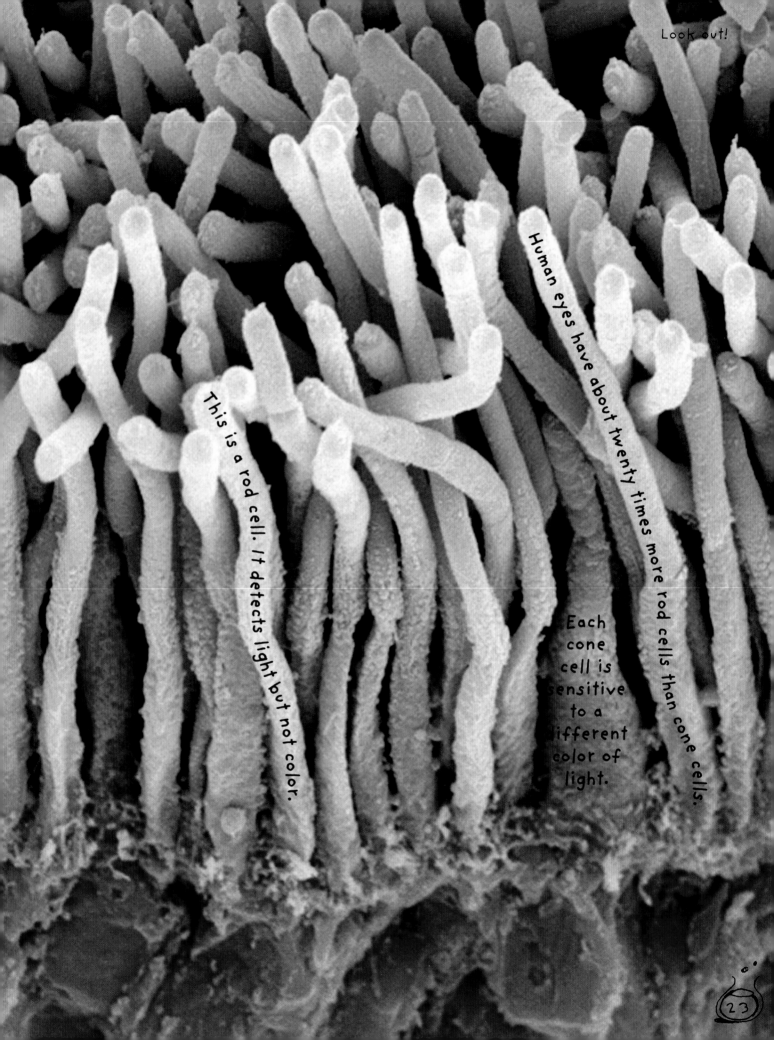

Look out!

This is a rod cell. It detects light but not color.

Human eyes have about twenty times more rod cells than cone cells.

Each cone cell is sensitive to a different color of light.

23

In the shades

The **SUN IS SHINING**, and you're scrunching up your eyes against the light. What you need is a pair of **SUNGLASSES!** They're the coolest way to protect your eyes from the damaging effects of sunlight.

BRIGHTNESS of light is measured in lumens. Your eyes are pretty comfortable up to about 3,500 LUMENS.

As light reflects off surfaces, the brightness increases. Light reflected off snow might reach as much as 12,000 LUMENS. That's why skiers wear sunglasses.

Brown lenses are good in hazy sunshine and places where there is lots of glare, such as on lakes or ski slopes.

Green lenses are good all around, but work particularly well in cloudy weather.

COLOR IN LENSES

Yellow and orange lenses improve contrast and are best for seeing on overcast days.

Gray is good in all weather—it's excellent for cycling when light changes as you pedal along.

UV RAYS—Lots of sunglasses offer
protection against UV RAYS. UV stands for
ULTRAVIOLET, which is a kind of light. We
can't actually see it, but it travels in sunlight
and can give us sunburn.

UV can have a similar
damaging effect on our eyes.
Both kinds (UVA and UVB)
can contribute to eye problems
including photokeratitis, which
is essentially eye sunburn.

MIRROR LENSES
are coated in a reflective
material. The coating is so
thin that it only reflects half
the light that hits the lens.
It lets the rest through.

Some sunglasses darken
in bright sunlight.
These are called
PHOTOCHROMIC.

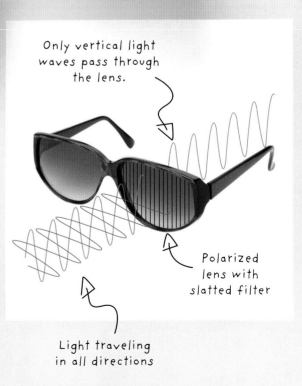

Only vertical light
waves pass through
the lens.

Polarized
lens with
slatted filter

Light traveling
in all directions

POLARIZED LENSES
Light travels in all directions.
Polarized lenses act as a kind
of slatted filter. They only
let through light that lines up
with the slats.

NOW TRY THIS!
You can test whether your sunglasses are
polarized by turning them through 90 degrees and
seeing whether a shiny horizontal surface becomes
brighter. If it does, your lenses are polarized.

Lava lamp

HAVE YOU EVER HEARD THE EXPRESSION, "WATER AND OIL DON'T MIX"? It's not just a saying—it's good science, and it's the reason you can make these colorful lava lamps at home. Try it and see.

ONE seltzer tablet for a small bottle, TWO for a large bottle.

HOW TO MAKE A LAVA LAMP

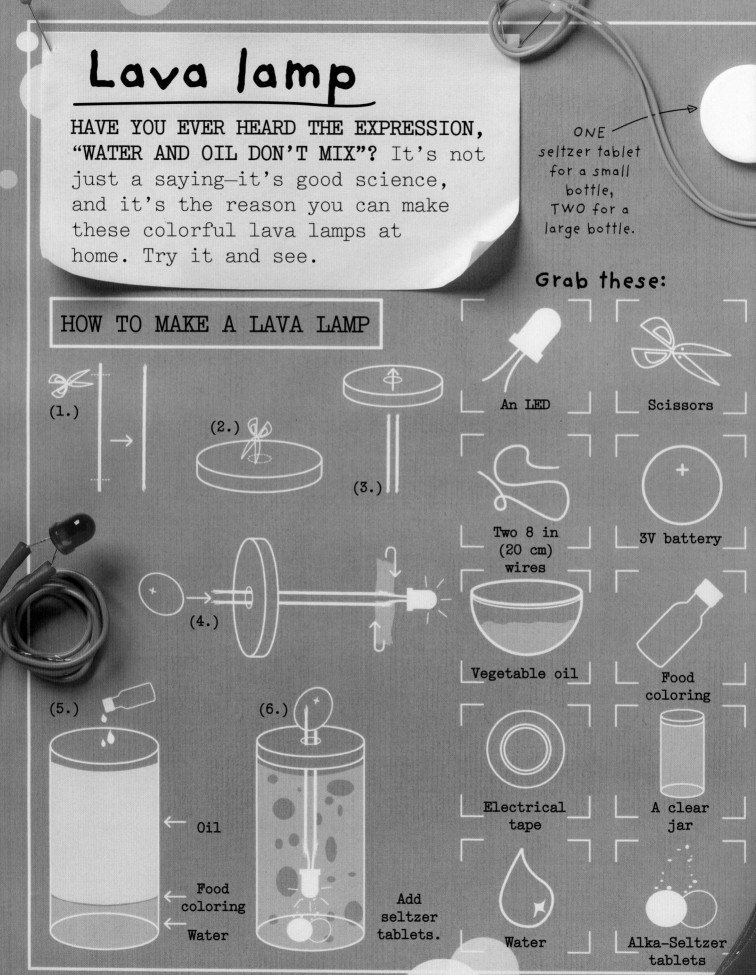

(1.)

(2.)

(3.)

(4.)

(5.)

Oil

Food coloring

Water

(6.)

Add seltzer tablets.

Grab these:

An LED

Scissors

Two 8 in (20 cm) wires

3V battery

Vegetable oil

Food coloring

Electrical tape

A clear jar

Water

Alka-Seltzer tablets

26

1. **Trim the plastic** casing from each end of two pieces of wire.

2. **Make a hole in the lid** of the jar using scissors (ask an adult to help with this).

3. **Push the wires through the hole** in the lid, so that they hang down.

4. **Wrap one end of** each wire around the wires of the LED. Tape together the LED and wires using electrical tape.

5. **Fill** about one-fifth of the jar with water. Top off with oil to just under the rim. Add a few drops of food coloring.

6. **Break up some** seltzer tablets. Drop them into the jar. Quickly put the lid on and connect the battery. If the LED doesn't light, turn the battery around.

How does it work?

Because the water and oil in this experiment don't mix, they form separate layers in the jar. The food coloring (which is mostly made of water) won't mix with the oil either.

Where do the bubbles come from? Seltzer tablets contain an acid (citric acid) and a base (sodium bicarbonate). Acids and bases react with each other. In this experiment, the acid and base mix together and react when the tablet dissolves in water. As part of the reaction, they give off bubbles of carbon dioxide gas, which is what makes blobs of colored water float upward.

It's perfectly safe for the wires and LED to hang into the oil in this experiment. But try not to get the battery wet.

If you don't fill your jar too full, you can leave off the lid. Just tape the LED in place.

WARNING:
Do not eat the Alka-Seltzers! An adult will need to supervise while you're using these tablets.

And remember: never put anything electrical near water if it is plugged into a wall socket.

Night lights

Man-made illuminations can't hold a candle to nature's own **LIGHT SHOW**. Tiny, electrically charged specks of matter constantly drift from the Sun toward Earth. These minute particles are magnetically drawn to the planet's poles. When they hit atoms in our atmosphere, their electrical energy is turned into light, creating an **AURORA**.

Light speed marshmallows

What kind of **HI-TECH** equipment do you need to measure the speed of light? Believe it or not, all you really need is an ordinary **MICROWAVE**, and a plate of **MARSHMALLOWS**.

MAKE SURE you ask Mom or Dad's permission before you use the microwave.

Grab these:

A microwave

A calculator

A bag of marshmallows

A ruler

A microwaveable plate

WARNING
Marshmallows can get very hot in the microwave. Let them cool before you eat any of them!

A plate or container with a flat surface will work best for this experiment.

① **Cover a plate** with marshmallows. Take the revolving turntable out of your microwave—it's important that the marshmallows stay still as they cook.

Don't cook your mallows for longer than 2 minutes.

2:00

② **Microwave the marshmallows** on a low heat. Check them regularly, and take them out as soon as melted dimples start to appear in some spots.

YUM
YUM!

The marshmallows will melt more in some places than in others.

③
Measure the shortest distance between the biggest dimples on the marshmallows; use metric and measure in METERS.

(For example 6 cm = 0.06 m)

How does it work?

Microwaves travel at the speed of light. They move in waves like this:

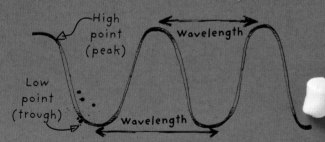

High point (peak)
Wavelength

Low point (trough)
Wavelength

The distance between two peaks or troughs is called a wavelength. The marshmallows will melt most at the peaks and troughs of the microwaves.

By measuring the distance between two melted parts, we can find out the distance between a peak and a trough. To find the wavelength you just need to **double that distance.**

The actual speed of light is **299,792,458 METERS/SECOND.**

Doing the math

Now you need to find out the **frequency** of the microwaves— which is how fast the waves move up and down. It should be written somewhere on the machine itself. It will be measured in **gigahertz**, or GHz, but you need it in hertz, so multiply by 1,000,000,000. Use a calculator to multiply the wavelength by the frequency, and you should get **the speed of light**!

Rainbow maker

This snazzy little gadget uses light in two very different ways. The **SOLAR PANEL** transforms light into power for a motor, which makes a crystal spin. And the **CRYSTAL** splits sunlight into **RAINBOWS**, which dance as it turns.

COLORS IN LIGHT

Isaac Newton, the genius who discovered gravity, also made some highly illuminating discoveries about light. He showed that normal sunlight is made up of many different colors of light, all **mixed together**. These confused colors can be separated by a **prism**.

The crystal of the rainbow maker contains lots of **prisms**. The prisms turn the mixed-up colors of sunlight into a **rainbow**.

When light travels into and out of a prism, it CHANGES DIRECTION.

Some colors change direction more than others. This **spreads out** the light into a rainbow.

Prism

This solar panel is made of silicon—the same stuff **sand** is made from.

How does a solar panel work?

① The silicon in a solar panel is shaped into two thin **wafers.**

② Sunlight can push **electrons** from one wafer to the other. Electrons are tiny specks of matter that carry an electrical charge.

③ The electrons pushed by the sun nudge along other electrons—and just like that, you have a flow of **electricity.**

Electricity powers this motor, which makes the crystal turn.

The Sun's light is the perfect energy source since it NEVER RUNS OUT! In the future, our homes may get their electricity from **solar power plants** with thousands upon thousands of solar panels.

These two solar speedsters are competing in the Alternative Energies Cup in Suzuka, Japan.

33

Ice bulb

A **GLOWING** ball of ice makes for a snazzy winter decoration—or if you're more **CREEPILY** inclined, you could create an eerie ice hand. This experiment is a little **TRICKY**, so get a friend to help.

Grab these:

Scissors

Two 8 in (20 cm) pieces of wire

An LED

Electrical tape

A plastic bowl

A 3V battery

A balloon

A rubber glove

Two rubber bands OR a food bag tie

Food coloring (optional)

Pins

① Use scissors to strip ½ in (1 cm) of plastic from the ends of each wire.

Strip two wires. Wrap one end of each wire around an LED pin. Fix them in place with electrical tape.

② It's a good idea to blow up the balloon first to stretch the rubber.

You could add a few drops of food coloring to the water.

Wrap the end of the balloon around a faucet and fill it halfway with water.

③ Try to get the LED in the middle of the balloon.

Push the LED into the balloon, leaving the ends of the wires hanging out.

34

Seal the end of the balloon with rubber bands or a food bag tie.

(4)

(5) **Put the balloon** in a plastic bowl and leave the bowl in the freezer overnight.
When the water has frozen, peel off the balloon. Tape the wires to a battery ...
AND THE ICE WILL LIGHT UP!
(If it doesn't light straight away, turn the battery around.)

ISN'T ICE COOL?

How does it work?

Light can travel through ice, but some wavelengths are absorbed more than others. Air bubbles and ice crystals in the ball will also reflect light out at different angles. Try making ice bulbs with different colored LEDs and see which works best.

HAUNTED HAND

Here's a **spooky** variation on the glowing ice ball. Use a **rubber glove** instead of a balloon, and make sure its fingers are straight when you freeze it.

YOUR ICE BULB will soon start to melt. Make sure you disconnect the battery before it gets wet.

35

Grab these:

Cardboard tube

Mirrored cardboard

Colored cardboard

Scissors

Shiny things

Tape

An LED

Clear container with lid

3V battery

Newspaper

Pencil

Kaleidoscope

LIGHT CAN'T GO AROUND CORNERS but it can bounce off things. And the things it bounces off best are MIRRORS. These give perfect reflections—and help make the ever-changing pattern inside this kaleidoscope.

MAKE A KALEIDOSCOPE

Once it's made, decorate your kaleidoscope with colored paper or paint.

(1.)

(2.)

(3.)

(4.)

(5.)

1. **Cut three rectangles** of mirrored cardboard as long as the cardboard tube. Tape the long sides together to make a long triangular shape. Make sure the mirrored sides all face inward.

2. **Push your mirrored triangle into the cardboard tube** and stuff the space between the cardboard and the tube with crumpled newspaper to hold it in place.

3. **Trace the end of the tube** onto the colored cardboard and cut out the circle. Tape it onto one end of the tube. Then use a pencil to stab a hole in the center—this will be your eyehole.

4. **Tape some LEDs** onto batteries with the short pin to the negative terminal (back) and the long pin to the positive terminal (front). Put these into a clear container that is about the same diameter as the tube. Add other objects—try beads, buttons, and shiny stars.

5. **Put the lid on the** container and tape it shut. Then tape it to the end of the kaleidoscope. Look through the hole and slowly rotate the tube. Watch the reflections change!

> LOOK INTO THE TUBE, ONE EYE AT A TIME.

How does it work?

Most objects reflect light, but what makes mirrors special is that their shiny surface bounces light back in exactly the same pattern that it hits them. A kaleidoscope bounces light between three mirrors arranged in a triangle. You see the reflected light as a complex pattern because of the way that the light's direction changes each time it hits an angled mirror.

NOW TRY THIS EXPERIMENT!
Make a kaleidoscope that has four or five mirrors and see what happens to the patterns.

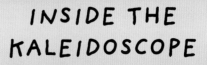

INSIDE THE KALEIDOSCOPE

Sunlight

It takes 8¹/₂ minutes for light from the Sun to reach the Earth. Its journey starts when hydrogen atoms get squashed together in the Sun's core. The light energy this produces takes a million years to travel from the core to the surface, and every square centimeter of the surface emits as much light as a 6,000 watt bulb.

Electric hoopla

Have you got the **SKILLS** to win this tricky game? To score, you just have to throw a hoop over a pole. But if the hoop hits the pole's metallic stripes, an LED lights and you **LOSE** your points.

Grab these:

Some aluminum foil

A paper plate

Two wires 8 in (20 cm) long and a wire 3 ft (1 m) long.

A cardboard tube

An LED

Scissors

A 3V battery

Electrical tape

Some uncoated wire (a coat hanger will do)

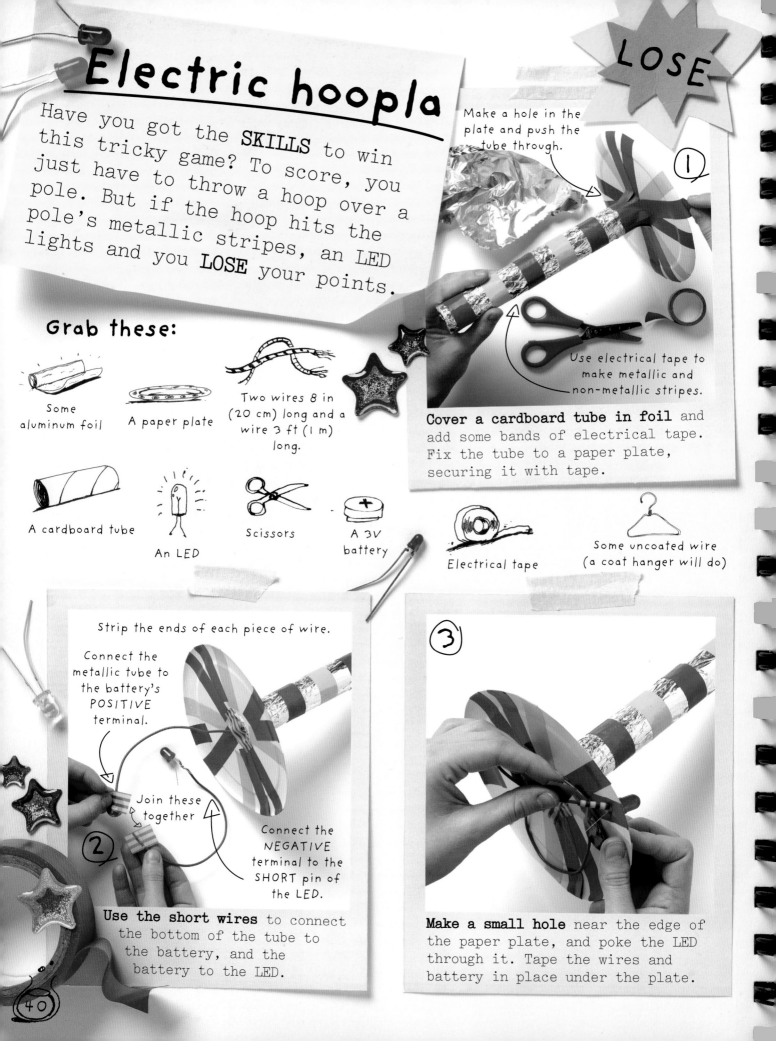

Make a hole in the plate and push the tube through.

①

Use electrical tape to make metallic and non-metallic stripes.

Cover a cardboard tube in foil and add some bands of electrical tape. Fix the tube to a paper plate, securing it with tape.

Strip the ends of each piece of wire.

Connect the metallic tube to the battery's POSITIVE terminal.

Join these together

②

Connect the NEGATIVE terminal to the SHORT pin of the LED.

Use the short wires to connect the bottom of the tube to the battery, and the battery to the LED.

③

Make a small hole near the edge of the paper plate, and poke the LED through it. Tape the wires and battery in place under the plate.

40

Hoop

4 Twist a piece of wire into a circle and tape the ends together.

Connect the long wire from the hoop to the LONG pin of the LED.

Make a hoop out of the uncoated wire. Wrap one end of the longest wire around the hoop, and wrap the other end around the LED. Tape in place.

5

Now tap the hoop against a metal-covered part of the striped pole. If the LED lights up, then you're ready to **play the game!**

OR TRY THIS: You could replace the LED in this experiment with a **buzzer**.

HOW TO PLAY

You can play this game alone or with a friend. Stand the striped pole on the floor, and step back a few paces. Then try to throw the hoop over the pole. You score 10 points if you can get the hoop over the pole **WITHOUT** lighting the LED. If you're playing with a friend, take turns throwing and see who can be the first to score 100 points.

WIN

How does it work?

When you touch the metal of the hoop to the metal of the pole, it completes an electrical circuit, allowing electrons to flow from the negative terminal of the battery to the positive terminal. As electricity flows round the circuit, it passes through the LED, making it light up.

Individual electrons (the tiny flecks of matter that carry electricity) are not fast-moving. In fact, they only move as fast as the minute hand on a clock. So why does the light go on immediately when you touch the hoop to the rod? You get instant power because the wires and foil are packed with electrons, and when one electron bumps into another, it passes its electrical charge on to the next one, like a runner in a relay race.

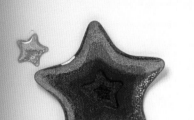

Glowing coral

These coral colonies use a **COLORFUL TRICK** to protect themselves from sunburn. Inside the coral are algae that provide them with food. When this algae gets too much harmful UV light, it dies, and so does the coral. But the coral's fluorescent coloring acts as a kind of **SUNSCREEN**, shielding the algae from UV rays.

Gel vision

Can gelatin play **TRICKS** with your **EYES**? Find out for yourself with these gel lenses. See what they do to the words and pictures on this page. It's truly wobble-tastic!

Grab these:

- Gelatin
- Knife
- Flashlight
- Plastic wrap
- Scissors
- Plastic bottles
- Paper towel
- Newspaper
- Vegetable oil
- Teaspoon
- Pitcher

MAKE GEL LENSES

(1.)

(2.)

Which colors work best?

(3.)

(4.)

CAN YOU SEE THE LINE CHANGE?

(5.)

Yuck!

Try it out on a picture or writing.

The white line distorts when the gel lens is placed over it.

LENSES ON A PICTURE

How does it work?

As light moves into a clear substance like gelatin, its path changes. Lenses with curved surfaces either bend light rays together or spread them over a large area.

A convex lens focuses light into a point and then spreads it out again. If your object is close to the crossing point it will look bigger.

A concave lens spreads light out. If you look through either side of this lens, an object on the other side will appear smaller.

1. Use scissors to cut the bottoms off some clean plastic drink bottles—these will be your gelatin molds.

2. Wipe vegetable oil around the inside of each mold.

3. Make some gelatin, using only HALF the amount of water given in the instructions. Pour the gelatin into your molds and put them in the fridge until the gelatin sets.

4. Tip out the molds onto plastic wrap—you may need to dip them in warm water to help the gelatin slide out.

5. Put the plastic wrap onto an old newspaper or comic book. Move the lens around by pulling on the plastic wrap. How does the lens affect the words? Do the words look bigger or smaller?

MORE GEL LENS EXPERIMENTS

Close the curtains, turn off the lights, and try shining a narrow light through each of your gel lenses. How does the light beam change as it passes through the lens? Does the lens focus the light or spread it out? Does the light change color?

Try using other curved containers to get different shaped lenses. Or pour gelatin into a balloon to get a double convex lens.

Glossary

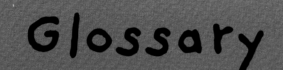

Acid a chemical that tastes sour, stings, or burns through other objects. Vinegar and lemon juice are both weak acids. Stronger acids can be very dangerous.

Antennae sense organs on an insect's head, used for touching and feeling things.

Atom a minute particle of matter that cannot be divided by chemical or mechanical means.

Aurora curtains of light that appear in the night sky near the poles, caused by electrically charged particles colliding with atoms in the atmosphere.

Base also called an alkali. A chemical that reacts with acids. Baking soda is a base.

Battery a device used to store electrical energy.

Circuit the path through which electricity flows when an electric device is switched on.

Conductor a substance that allows electricity to flow through it. All metals are conductors.

Crystal a solid that has a regular shape and flat faces that are arranged symmetrically.

Electricity a form of energy that can be transmitted by wires.

Electron a particle with a negative charge that orbits the nucleus of an atom.

Fluorescence the light given off when a substance absorbs some light energy and emits the rest at a lower frequency.

Frequency the number of wavelengths of light that pass a given point in a second.

Insulator a substance that doesn't transmit electricity. Wood, plastic, rubber, and glass are good insulators.

Lens a transparent material that has been shaped to have one or two curved surfaces.

Light a form of energy that travels in waves. It includes radio waves, microwaves, ultraviolet, visible, infrared, X-rays, and gamma rays.

Microwaves very short wavelengths of light energy that are used in some ovens.

Optical fiber an extremely thin glass or plastic thread that carries light.

Polarization filtering light waves so that only those traveling in one direction pass through.

Prism a transparent object with flat, polished surfaces that splits white light into colors.

Quartz a medium hard mineral made of silicon dioxide that forms six-sided crystals.

Reflection the change in direction of a light wave when it hits a surface.

Retina the light sensitive surface at the back of the eye that receives the image formed by the lens.

Semiconductor a material that is not as good at transmitting electricity as a conductor, but will allow it to flow under certain conditions.

Spectrum the series of colors of visible light, ranging from red to violet.

Wavelength the distance between two peaks or troughs of a wave.